"Our political way of life is by the
and of course presupposes the existenc
universe, and a rule of right and wrong,
man, preceding all institutions of human society and of g...

— John Quincy Adams

John Quincy Adams

President of the United States, 1825-1829

Engraved by W. Wellstood after a photograph by Mathew Brady.

Reproduced from THE DICTIONARY OF AMERICAN PORTRAITS
published by Dover Publications, Inc., in 1967

About the Cover Photo

A portion of Caerphilly Castle, which is the largest castle in Wales. The author, in a red shirt, stands on a bridge above one of the moats at the gate in one of the lower outer walls. This massive citadel replaced a small Roman fort after the Roman Empire collapsed. Europe contains hundreds of these kinds of stone castles. The expense of building them was enormous, and contributed much to the impoverishment of the people. Today these castles are a reminder of how much the people of the Middle Ages feared their neighbors after law was destroyed.

About the "Uncle Eric" Series

The "Uncle Eric" series of books is written by Richard J. Maybury for young and old alike. Using the epistolary style of writing (using letters to tell a story), Mr. Maybury plays the part of an economist writing a series of letters to his niece or nephew. Using stories and examples, he gives interesting and clear explanations of topics that are generally thought to be too difficult for anyone but experts.

Mr. Maybury warns, "beware of anyone who tells you a topic is above you or better left to experts. Many people are twice as smart as they think they are but they've been intimidated into believing some topics are above them. You can understand almost anything if it is explained well."

The series is called UNCLE ERIC'S MODEL OF HOW THE WORLD WORKS (see pages 6-9 of this book). In the series, Mr. Maybury writes from the political, legal and economic viewpoint of America's Founders. The books can be read in any order and have been written to stand alone. To get the most from each one, however, Mr. Maybury suggests the following order of reading.

Uncle Eric's Model of How the World Works

Uncle Eric Talks About Personal, Career and Financial Security

Whatever Happened to Penny Candy?

Whatever Happened to Justice?

Are You Liberal? Conservative? or Confused?

Ancient Rome: How It Affects You Today

Evaluating Books: What Would Thomas Jefferson Think About This?

The Money Mystery

The Clipper Ship Strategy

The Thousand Year War in the Mideast

World War I

World War II

(Study guides available or forthcoming for above titles.)

An "Uncle Eric" Book

Ancient Rome

How It Affects You Today

by Richard J. Maybury
("Uncle Eric")

published by
Bluestocking Press
P.O. Box 1014 • Dept. AR
Placerville • CA • 95667-1014

Printed in the United States of America.

Edited by Jane A. Williams

Library of Congress Cataloging-in-Publication Data
Maybury, Rick.
    Ancient Rome : how it affects you today / by Richard J. Maybury ("Uncle Eric").
        p. cm. -- (An "Uncle Eric" book)
    Includes bibliographical references and index.
    ISBN 0-942617-22-3 (alk. paper)
    1. Rome--Politics and government--30 B.C.-576 A.D. 2. World politics--20th century. 3. Civilization, Modern--Roman influences. I. Title. II. Series: Maybury, Rick. "Uncle Eric" book.
DG273.M39   1995
909.82--dc20   95-14032
                                                              CIP

Published by   **Bluestocking Press**
Post Office Box 1014
Dept. AR
Placerville, CA 95667-1014

To my publisher, Jane Williams,
who had the foresight and tenacity
to resurrect Uncle Eric.

Uncle Eric's Model
of How the World Works

What is a model? In his book UNCLE ERIC TALKS ABOUT PERSONAL, CAREER AND FINANCIAL SECURITY, Richard Maybury (Uncle Eric) explains that one of the most important things you can teach children, or learn yourself, is:

"Models are how we think, they are how we understand how the world works. As we go through life we build these very complex pictures in our minds of how the world works, and we're constantly referring back to them— matching incoming data against our models. That's how we make sense of things. One of the most important uses for models is in sorting incoming information to decide if it's important or not.

"In most schools, models are never mentioned because the teachers are unaware of them. One of the most dangerous weaknesses in traditional education is that it contains no model for political history. Teachers teach what they were taught — and no one ever mentioned models to them, so they don't teach them to their students. For the most part, children are just loaded down with collections of facts that they are made to memorize. Without good models, children have no way to know which facts are important and which are not. Students leave school thinking history is a senseless waste of time. Then, deprived of the real lessons of history, the student is vulnerable."

The question is, which models to teach. Mr. Maybury says, "the two models that I think are crucially important for everyone to learn are economics and law."

WHATEVER HAPPENED TO PENNY CANDY? explains the economic model, which is based on Austrian economics, the most free-market of all economic models. WHATEVER HAPPENED TO JUSTICE? explains the legal model and shows the connection between rational law and economic progress. The legal model is the old British Common Law — or Natural Law. The original principles on which America was founded were those of the old British Common Law.

These two books, PENNY CANDY and JUSTICE, provide the overall model of how human civilization works, especially the world of money.

Once the model is understood, read ARE YOU LIBERAL? CONSERVATIVE? OR CONFUSED? which explains political philosophies relative to Uncle Eric's Model — and makes a strong case for consistency to that model, no exceptions.

Next, read ANCIENT ROME: HOW IT AFFECTS YOU TODAY which shows what happens when a society ignores Uncle Eric's Model and embraces fascism.

To help you locate books and authors generally in agreement with these economic and legal models, Mr. Maybury wrote EVALUATING BOOKS: WHAT WOULD THOMAS JEFFERSON THINK ABOUT THIS? which provides guidelines for selecting books that are consistent with the principles of America's founders. You can apply these guidelines to books, movies, news commentators, current events — to any spoken or written medium.

Further expanding on the economic model is THE MONEY MYSTERY which explains the hidden force affecting your career, business and investments. Some economists refer to this force as velocity, others to money demand. Whichever term is used, it is one of the least understood forces affecting your life. Knowing about velocity and money demand not only gives you an understanding of history that few others have, it prepares you to understand and avoid pitfalls in your career, business and investments. THE MONEY MYSTERY is the first sequel to WHATEVER HAPPENED TO PENNY CANDY? and provides essential background for getting the most from THE CLIPPER SHIP STRATEGY.

THE CLIPPER SHIP STRATEGY is the practical application of MONEY MYSTERY and PENNY CANDY. Conventional wisdom says that when the government expands the money supply, the money descends on the economy in a uniform blanket. This is wrong, the money is injected into specific locations causing hot spots or "cones." Mr. Maybury explains his system for tracking and profiting from the cones. This book is the second sequel to WHATEVER HAPPENED TO PENNY CANDY? and should be read after THE MONEY MYSTERY.

THE THOUSAND YEAR WAR IN THE MIDEAST: HOW IT AFFECTS YOU TODAY explains how events on the other side of the world a thousand years ago can affect us more than events in our hometowns today. In the 1970s, '80s and '90s, the Thousand Year War has been the cause of great shocks to the investment markets, including the oil embargoes, the Iranian hostage crisis, the Iraq-Kuwait war, and the Caucasus Wars over the Caspian Sea oil basin — and it is likely to remain so for decades to come. Forewarned is forearmed. You must understand where this war is leading to manage your career, business and investments.

The economic crisis and turmoil in the stock market that began in 1997 affects our daily lives profoundly, and probably will continue to do so for years to come. This disturbance had its origin in foreign nations — nations in which the U.S. government intervenes on a regular basis. The justification for these interventions grew out of the Hollywood movie view of World War II. How accurate is this view? In his forthcoming book, WORLD WAR II: HOW IT AFFECTS YOU TODAY, Richard Maybury gives the other side of the story, the side you are not likely to get anywhere else.

Study Guide Available

A BLUESTOCKING GUIDE: ANCIENT ROME

BY JANE A. WILLIAMS

based on Richard J. Maybury's book
ANCIENT ROME: HOW IT AFFECTS YOU TODAY

Study Guides are published by Bluestocking Press (see order information on page 96 of this book). Study Guides are also available or forthcoming for other "Uncle Eric" books. For information, phone: 530-621-1123 or 800-959-8586.

The "Uncle Eric" books can be read in any order and have been written to stand alone. But to get the most from each one, Mr. Maybury suggests the following order of reading:

Uncle Eric's Model
of How the World Works

Book 1. UNCLE ERIC TALKS ABOUT PERSONAL, CAREER AND FINANCIAL SECURITY.

Book 2. WHATEVER HAPPENED TO PENNY CANDY? *A Fast, Clear and Fun Explanation of the Economics You Need for Success in Your Career, Business and Investments.* (Study Guide available.)

Book 3. WHATEVER HAPPENED TO JUSTICE?

Book 4. ARE YOU LIBERAL? CONSERVATIVE? OR CONFUSED?

Book 5. ANCIENT ROME: *How It Affects You Today.* (Study Guide available.)

Book 6. EVALUATING BOOKS: *What Would Thomas Jefferson Think About This?*

Book 7. THE MONEY MYSTERY: *The Hidden Force Affecting Your Career, Business and Investments.*

Book 8. THE CLIPPER SHIP STRATEGY: *For Success in Your Career, Business and Investments.*

Book 9: THE THOUSAND YEAR WAR IN THE MIDEAST: *How It Affects You Today.*

Book 10: WORLD WAR II: *How It Affects You Today.* Future title.

Contents

Note to Reader

Throughout each "Uncle Eric" book, whenever a word that appears in the glossary is introduced in the text, it is displayed in a **bold typeface.**

Author's Disclosure

For reasons I do not understand, writers today are supposed to be objective. Few disclose the viewpoints or opinions they use to decide what information is important and what is not, or what shall be presented or omitted.

I do not adhere to this standard and make no pretense of being objective. I am biased in favor of liberty and free markets, and proud of it. So, I disclose my viewpoint which you will find explained in detail in my newsletter and my other books.[1]

For those who have not yet read these publications, I call my viewpoint Juris Naturalism (pronounced *jur*-es *nach*-e-re-liz-em, sometimes abbreviated JN) meaning the belief in a natural law that is higher than any government's law. Here are six quotes from America's founders that help to describe this viewpoint:

"...all men are created equal, that they are endowed by their Creator with certain unalienable rights."
— Declaration of Independence, 1776

"The natural rights of the colonists are these: first, a right to life; second to liberty; third to property; together with the right to support and defend them in the best manner they can."
— Samuel Adams, 1772

---

[1] See RICHARD MAYBURY'S EARLY WARNING REPORT newsletter, published by Henry-Madison Research, Box 1616 AR, Rocklin, CA, 95677, and his books (see pgs. 8-9), published by Bluestocking Press, Placerville, CA.

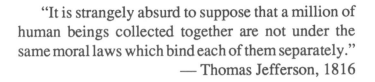

"It is strangely absurd to suppose that a million of human beings collected together are not under the same moral laws which bind each of them separately."
— Thomas Jefferson, 1816

"A wise and frugal government, which shall restrain men from injuring one another, which shall leave them otherwise free to regulate their own pursuits of industry and improvement, and shall not take from the mouth of labor the bread it has earned. This is the sum of good government."
— Thomas Jefferson, 1801

"Not a place on earth might be so happy as America. Her situation is remote from all the wrangling world, and she has nothing to do but to trade with them."
— Thomas Paine, 1776

"The great rule of conduct for us, in regard to foreign nations, is, in extending our commercial relations, to have with them as little political connection as possible."
— George Washington, 1796

George
Washington

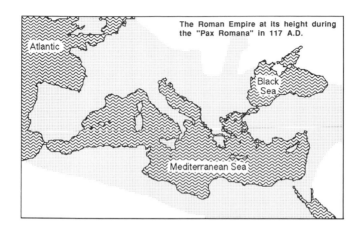

The Roman Empire at its height during the "Pax Romana" in 117 A.D.

Atlantic

Black Sea

Mediterranean Sea

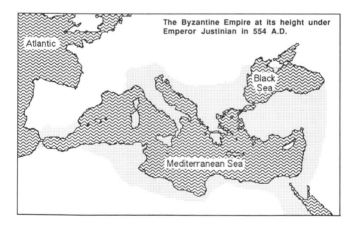

The Byzantine Empire at its height under Emperor Justinian in 554 A.D.

Atlantic

Black Sea

Mediterranean Sea

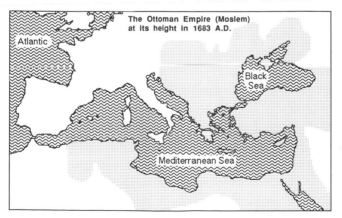

The Ottoman Empire (Moslem) at its height in 1683 A.D.

Atlantic

Black Sea

Mediterranean Sea

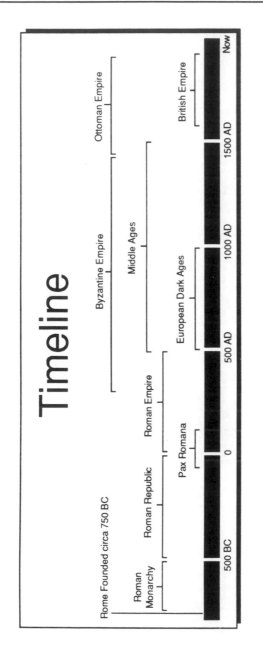

Timeline

Rome Founded circa 750 BC

Roman Monarchy

Roman Republic

Roman Empire

Pax Romana

Byzantine Empire

Ottoman Empire

Middle Ages

European Dark Ages

British Empire

500 BC | 0 | 500 AD | 1000 AD | 1500 AD | Now

The Pax Romana was the period in which Roman power was at its zenith. Romans had conquered and now ruled the entire Mediterranean world. They enforced peace by ruthlessly punishing war and rebellion by any who wished to declare independence. Today the Pax Romana remains an inspiration for politicians everywhere.

1

History Repeats

Dear Chris,

You mentioned that after reading my previous letters[2] about law and economics you can see how important it is for you to know some history. Since you now understand these economic and legal models, you are definitely ready to tackle some history. And, as usual, I'm going to approach this in a way that isn't normally found in your history textbooks today.

I'm sure you've heard the old proverb, history repeats. Or, those that forget history are doomed to repeat it. Not many people would argue with the wisdom of these proverbs. A question you might logically ask is, "Why do we forget our history?"

I believe one big reason is that most people today lack the tools to understand it. Without the background in law and

---

[2] Uncle Eric is referring to WHATEVER HAPPENED TO PENNY CANDY? (about economics) and WHATEVER HAPPENED TO JUSTICE? (about law) published by Bluestocking Press, PO Box 1014, Placerville, CA. In WHATEVER HAPPENED TO PENNY CANDY? Uncle Eric uses historical events from Ancient Rome to explain economic principles, making it an excellent companion book to ANCIENT ROME: HOW IT AFFECTS YOU TODAY.

economics that you've learned from our previous correspondence, you would have no way to make sense of whatever history you study. It would be nothing but a collection of names and dates of presidents, kings and wars, with no lessons to teach. In other words, it would be all trivia, unrelated data, with no meaningful use.

You know from my previous letters that American history is important to us, but world history is, too. I am often amazed at how events on the other side of the world a thousand years ago affect us more than events in our hometowns today. And, they affect us not in a subtle or general way, but very immediately on a day to day basis.

For example, do you remember the Iraq-Kuwait war in 1990? It not only brought the deaths of 293 Americans, it caused oil prices to double and the stock market to fall 19%. This stemmed from the conflicts between the Christian and Moslem worlds that began during the Middle Ages. Because my work requires me to study these matters[3], I (and others) saw this war coming a full year before it happened. In August 1989 I gave a speech[4] warning about it. Investors who took my advice made handsome profits.

That's just one example of why understanding history can be important to us.

---

[3] To read more about the conflicts between the Christian and Moslem worlds that began during the Middle Ages, read Richard Maybury's "Uncle Eric" book THE THOUSAND YEAR WAR IN THE MIDEAST: HOW IT AFFECTS YOU TODAY. In addition to writing Uncle Eric books, when Mr. Maybury refers to "my work" he is also referring to his investment newsletter, RICHARD MAYBURY'S EARLY WARNING REPORT, published by Henry-Madison Research, Box 1616-AR, Rocklin, CA, 95677.

[4] On August 10, 1989, Richard Maybury gave a speech to the Eris Society in Aspen, Colorado predicting the Iraq-Kuwait war and the effects on the investment markets. On August 2, 1990, Iraq attacked Kuwait.

Here are more thoughts about the importance of knowing history.

"The disadvantage of men not knowing the past is that they do not know the present. History is a hill or high point of vantage, from which alone men see the town in which they live or the age in which they are living."   — C.K. Chesterton, 1933

"To be ignorant of what occurred before you were born is to remain always a child." — Cicero, 46 B.C.

"That men do not learn very much from the lessons of history is the most important of all the lessons that history has to teach."   — Aldous Huxley, 1959

"History, by apprizing them of the past, will enable them to judge of the future; it will avail them of the experience of other times and other nations; it will qualify them as judges of the actions and designs of men."   —Thomas Jefferson, 1781

"We can chart our future clearly and wisely only when we know the path which has led to the present." — Adlai Stevenson, 1952

"Human history becomes more and more a race between education and catastrophe." — H.G. Wells, 1920

"We have need of history in its entirety, not to fall back into it, but to see if we can escape from it." — Jose' Ortega Y Gasset, 1930

Chris, as you may gather from Gasset's remark, we are, in a sense, prisoners of history. Our present is the result of the past, and our future will be the result of the present. But we are not helpless, we can keep the mistakes of history from repeating. I like this insight:

> "The history of free men is never really written by chance but by choice — their choice."
> — Dwight D. Eisenhower, 1956

So, to build a better future we need to know how we got where we are today. As you may have gathered from my previous letters, a lot of it has to do with the **Roman Empire**, especially what I call the **Roman disease**. So let's get started, you'll be amazed. In my next letter we'll again be looking at coins, and at many other things you see in your everyday life. As you read, it will also be helpful to have a good globe or atlas nearby. I especially recommend the TIMES ATLAS OF WORLD HISTORY published by Hammond. Until then, remember that those who read and understand history have a mighty advantage over those who do not.

Uncle Eric

2

The Roman Disease
that Stalks the Markets

Dear Chris,

You said you're glad we'll be looking at coins again.[5] Good. Wise and informed money management is essential in today's world. Let me explain.

Investment values are determined mostly by trends in the economy, and trends in the economy are determined mostly by politics. To know what's coming in the investment markets we must first know what's coming in politics, especially world politics.

The political trend that has dominated the world for 2,000 years, including the investment markets, remains almost unrecognized. I call it the Roman disease, and I'll introduce you to it in this and the next few letters.

Sometimes the Roman disease goes dormant for brief periods but over the past twenty centuries it has always

---

[5] Uncle Eric first discussed coins and money with Chris in WHATEVER HAPPENED TO PENNY CANDY? published by Bluestocking Press, Placerville, CA, 1993.

resurfaced as deadly as ever. It may now be returning to demolish the nations of the former Soviet Empire. More about that later. For now you need to know that the Roman disease could be the strongest influence on our businesses, careers and investments for the rest of our lives. Here's the story.

Reach into your pocket or purse for a penny and a Roosevelt dime. If you are fortunate enough to have a Mercury dime (silver) dated 1919 to 1945, get that too.

On the back of the penny you'll see the Lincoln memorial. Note the style of the architecture. Like the US Capitol Building, it is Greco-Roman, meaning a combination of Greek and Roman. You'll also see the motto "E Pluribus Unum" which is Latin for "out of many, one." Latin was the language of the Roman Empire, and this motto applauds political unity.

The Mercury dime closely resembles a Roman silver denarius. On the back you'll see a cylindrical Roman object

This is the basic style of Roman architecture. Signifying statism, it is typical of government buildings throughout western civilization. The style is derived from temples to mythical gods.

Capitol buildings in the US use Roman architecture.

called a **fasces**. This was a bundle of wooden rods bound together by red-colored bands. In ancient Rome the fasces was fixed to a wooden pole, with an ax at the top or side. It symbolized the unification of the people under a single government.

The ax suggested what would happen to anyone who didn't obey the government.

The Roman fasces is the origin of the word **fascism**.

Both dimes also show laurel leaves. I will tell you about them later.

These seemingly trivial images are crucially important to our businesses, careers and investments. Hard to believe? Read on.

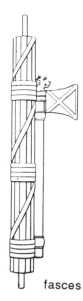

fasces

Western civilization is littered with references to the Roman Empire. Its coins, architecture, language and legal and economic theories are so filled with Romanisms that we no longer see them for what they are. They've become our mental furniture, they are so much a part of us that few people today question the need for a powerful central government.

ROMAN LAW

Whenever Uncle Eric uses the term Roman law, he means Roman law during the Roman Empire, not during the Republic.

Now, Chris, what I'm about to say is very important for you to understand. **Roman law**[6] during the Roman Empire assumes the individual's rights are granted by the the state (by government) and laws can be made up by lawmakers. Under Roman law, the state is supreme, and

---

[6] Whenever Uncle Eric uses the term Roman law, he means Roman law during the Roman Empire not during the Roman Republic.

rights are granted or erased whenever lawmakers decide. This philosophy is sometimes called **statism**. Its basic premise is that there is no law higher than the government's law.

Roman politicians were not the first to invent statism but they did such an effective job of applying it that the Roman Empire has become the guiding star for politicians everywhere. Statists see the **"Pax Romana"** — the period in which Rome dominated the Mediterranean world — as the good old days. That was when the known world was **"unified,"** symbolized by the fasces.

What does unified mean?

Many historians today are fond of calling any king who unified his nation, a great man. Examples are Russia's Peter the Great and Alexander the Great of Macedonia and Greece.

Remember the ax that topped the fasces? We have all been taught that political unity is good. But **political unity** really means a large, powerful government that all are forced to obey. In most cases, unifying a country means conquering anyone who wishes to be independent. Czar Peter, like most other "great" rulers, was a ruthless killer. But his murder and mayhem are often glossed over because in today's world the Roman ideal of "unity" is accepted almost without question.

Chris, in my next letter we'll continue exploring the Roman ideal of unity. Until then remember that Roman ideas and symbols are now so much a part of our culture that we no longer recognize them for what they are.

Nazi standards copied the standards of the Roman legions.

                    Uncle Eric

3

The Roman Model

Dear Chris,

The Roman disease is why Europeans are the most war-like people on earth. Rome dominated Europe, and Europeans have inherited the Roman disease. Under statism, Europe has given us both world wars, the Thirty Years War, the Hundred Years War, the Crusades and many others. Statism is a philosophy of conquest. All must obey, or else.

Empire is the European obsession. The German word **Kaiser** and the Russian word **Czar** both mean **Caesar**. Otto the First ruled the "Holy Roman" Empire. Napoleon had himself crowned emperor. Hitler and Mussolini... but I'll tell you about them in a future letter.

What is important for us and our money is that most politicians today make decisions on the basis of the **Roman model**. They want a powerful central government that can tax and control everything, watchdog everyone's business, and fight wars anywhere on earth. The effect on the economy and our money has been profound, and will continue to be for years to come.

Under the Roman model, laws change continually. Business people and investors cannot plan ahead because the ground rules, and flows of money channeled by these rules, are forever changing. As you know from my previous sets of letters, legal instability brings economic instability.

Like the Roman government, politicians today love "unity," meaning, "everyone follows our orders or else." This was the Pax Romana — the Roman Peace — do as you are told, don't make waves, or be hauled away in chains. Wars and rebellions by those who wished to declare independence during the Pax Romana were ruthlessly crushed.

In the United States, the Roman model has been adopted by both sides of the political spectrum. Democrat Bill Clinton, for instance, made no secret of his desire to tax and control our work, our medical care, anything economic. Republican George Bush was invited to a war[7] on the other side of the world and he rushed to join.

Rome is the model for the United Nations, a super-government that seeks to create a Pax Romana for the whole world.

America was founded on the **common law** model which assumes there is a higher law than any government's law. But over the decades this model has been gradually subverted and replaced by Roman law. It isn't always called Roman law but this is what it is, the supremacy of the state. Unity. Obedience. Empire. Power. Justice is whatever lawmakers say it is.

The destruction of common law should not be surprising. Political power corrupts. Common law hates political power and tries to neutralize it. Roman law embraces it and seeks to expand it.

In ancient Rome the obvious absurdity of humans making up laws was neatly sidestepped by the assertion that the emperor was divine.

---

[7] Iraq-Kuwait War, 1990-91.

*The Arch of Triumph
of Emperor Constantine in Rome*

*Napoleon's Arc de Triomphe in Paris
(1806) and the Washington Arch in New
York (1889) are two of the many Trium-
phal Arches that copy Roman arches.*

In America today stat-
ists have yet to confront this
problem but we can see the
direction things are headed.
Many government buildings
have the look and feel of
cathedrals.

Mercury and Roosevelt
dimes show sprays of laurel
leaves. Roman emperors
were crowned with laurel
leaves.

The last hurrah of the
common law was the 1945
Nuremburg trials. There the
Nazi defendants pled not
guilty — they had been following the orders of their
government. The judges
sentenced them to hang, explaining that there is "a higher
duty" than anything our governments can impose on us.

But all this has been swept away now, and replaced by
the Roman model in which "I was just following orders" is a
valid defense. We hear this from government bureaucrats
every day. No matter what they do to hurt us, their defense is
always, "Hey, I'm just doing my job." They are good
Romans.

That's what we are all taught today in our schools, movies,
TV and elsewhere. The Roman model is now America's
model.

In Rome's early years, around 600 B.C., the kings claimed
to have divine or magical powers, one of which was the

power to make up laws. Kings were chosen by a group of soothsayers called **augurs**. In a kind of black magic, the augurs would talk with the gods and get their advice about who to make king. Thus the king was **"inaugurated"** — given magical powers — a process still used today. **Inauguration** is the ceremony in which a government official is put in office either to make up laws or to enforce these laws.

In its most virulent form, the Roman model is fascism. In PLANNED CHAOS, economist Ludwig von Mises wrote that fascism "claimed to be the gospel" of the "resurrected spirit of ancient Rome."

Today it usually isn't called fascism. Hitler and Mussolini gave fascism a bad name. In 1946 the fasces was removed from the dime. But the underlying Roman ideas are still dominant in Washington and every other major capitol — especially now in East Europe and the former USSR.

Understanding the Roman disease has been important for managing our businesses and investments for decades. And now, with the fast resurgence of the disease in the former Soviet Empire, and its growth in the United States, our understanding of it is critical. I fear we are returning to the 1930s when the Roman model was applied with a vengeance. Under the basic fascist principle that powerholders should do whatever appears necessary, the US government gave us the New Deal programs that were the beginning of today's massive tax-and-spend bureaucracy.

Incidentally, it is one of the great paradoxes of human history that as the British people were evolving the finest system of common law ever known, their government was history's strongest advocate of the Roman model, conquering people on every continent. At it's height a hundred years ago, the British Empire controlled 16 million square miles of land and 500 million people. That was more than a quarter of all the land on earth and nearly a third of the world population. The British Empire was and still is the envy of every powerseeker.

Chris, in my next letter we will revisit the 1930s, then look at what's happening today.

Until then remember that Roman law is the opposite of common law — it assumes there is no law higher than the government's law — and it is the basis of all legal systems today. It is also the basis of fascism.

Uncle Eric

Until World War II, images of President Abraham Lincoln were often accompanied by a fasces. An example is this statue in Lincoln, Nebraska erected in 1912.

In Washington DC's Lincoln Memorial erected in 1920, Lincoln's chair displays two fasces. Many Americans have been taught that Lincoln was America's greatest president. Why do you suppose he was depicted with the fasces? Why were the fasces not shown with axes, and why were the fasces eliminated entirely after World War II?

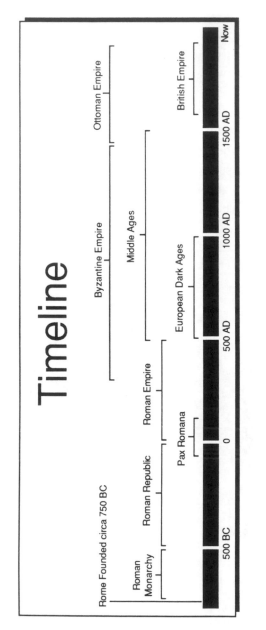

Timeline

Rome Founded circa 750 BC

Roman Monarchy

Roman Republic

Pax Romana

Roman Empire

Byzantine Empire

Ottoman Empire

Middle Ages

European Dark Ages

British Empire

500 BC | 0 | 500 AD | 1000 AD | 1500 AD | Now

The Pax Romana was the period in which Roman power was at its zenith. Romans had conquered and now ruled the entire Mediterranean world. They enforced peace by ruthlessly punishing war and rebellion by any who wished to declare independence. Today the Pax Romana remains an inspiration for politicians everywhere.

4

Hitler and Mussolini

Dear Chris,

When I write about the Roman disease I'm reminded of an old Kingston Trio song about mankind's endless wars; it goes something like, "the French hate the Germans, the Germans hate the Dutch, and I don't like anybody very much."

Much of this hatred and war is due to the popularity of the Roman model of government. Here's the story.

Roman civilization in Europe lasted roughly 1250 years. It can be divided into three parts.

The first two and one-half centuries until about 500 B.C. was the **Roman Monarchy** when statism was the system. This was when inauguration was invented.

The next five centuries until about the year 0 were the **Roman Republic**. This was the era of abundance and expansion under an early form of common law, which had partly replaced statism.

From 0 to 500 A.D. was the **Roman Empire**, when statism returned with a vengeance. This was the era of rampant lawmaking, plus the "bread and circuses" welfare state, endless war, crushing taxes and runaway inflation.

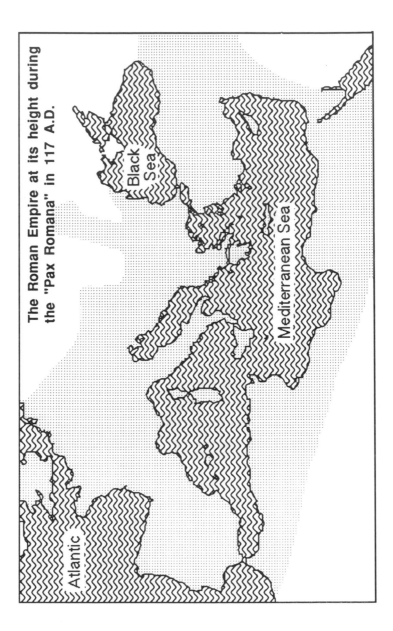

The Roman Empire at its height during the "Pax Romana" in 117 A.D.

Black Sea

Mediterranean Sea

Atlantic

The Pax Romana, which lasted about 200 years beginning in 31 B.C., was the period of the greatest extent of the Empire. The common law had created enough wealth that the government could collect enormous taxes to finance its army, forts and roads, and conquer the whole Mediterranean world.

But the taxes, inflation and made-up laws eventually killed the goose that laid the golden eggs. By 500 A.D., Roman civilization in Europe was dead and the **Dark Ages** had begun. In future letters I'll tell you the story of this decline. Like the former Soviet Empire today, Europe splintered into small states ruled by independent mafia chieftans called feudal lords. In Germany alone these tiny states numbered some 300, and they fought with each other continually.

The bloodshed and poverty of the Dark Ages were so horrifying that later scholars mourned the loss of the Roman Empire and pined for its return. Not understanding the connection between common law, peace and prosperity, these scholars were unable to identify the Roman disease. The result: a desire to return to what caused the trouble in the first place — a powerful central state. History repeats. Politicians jumped on the bandwagon and they've been on it ever since. Deep in his soul, every powerseeker is a Caesar trying to recreate the Pax Romana. He may not understand this — he may know nothing of history — but he has picked up the subliminal messages that surround us, and tries to embellish them and pass them on. He erects buildings, mints coins, makes up laws, raises armies and does whatever else he can to bring his statist dreams to life. I call this the Roman disease, and in the 1930s it reached fever pitch.

Mussolini was first. In 1919, he formed his fascist organization, The Fascisti, and adopted the trappings of the old Roman Empire. It was so popular that in just three years he took over Italy.

Hitler's gang copied him. Mussolini claimed to want only what was best for his homeland, so did Hitler. Mussolini was building a brave new empire, so was Hitler. Mussolini wrapped his movement in pageantry, color and mysticism, and so did Hitler.

It was all an attempt to recreate Rome. Watching his troops march, Mussolini renamed the **goose step** the Roman step.

In the throes of the world-wide Great Depression of the 1930s, it electrified the impoverished voters and gave them hope.

Note this. Neither Mussolini nor Hitler rose to power on the promise to start a new world war. They had plans to redraw the map of Europe but, for the most part, their followers ignored this. The two fascists became popular by promising to revive their economies and make their nations great again. It was "For the Fatherland!"

History repeats. In January, 1994, Russia's new fascist leader Vladimir Zhirinovsky declared, "We will have our great fatherland!" Asked about their opponents, one of his followers told the WALL STREET JOURNAL, "If Zhirinovsky would tell us to do so, we would kill them like flies." In the FINANCIAL TIMES of London, Zhirinovsky was quoted as saying, "The world should think twice before opposing us — after all, is it really desirable to have a third world war?"

As far as I know, fascism is the only philosophy that is really no philosophy at all. Fascism, as you may recall from our previous letters, emphasizes action instead of ideas. It shuns all theories and systems. Its fundamental premise is

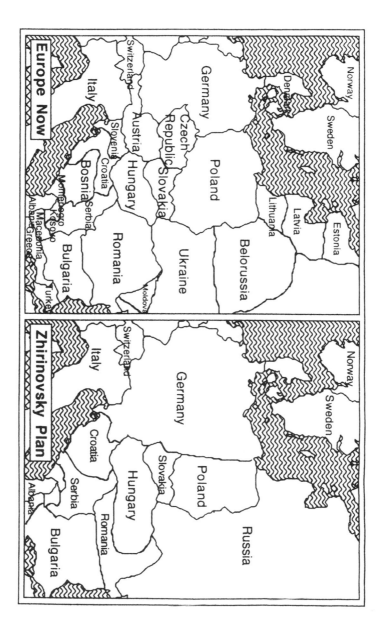

that right and wrong are just matters of opinion, rulers should do whatever appears necessary. This is the only guiding rule, do whatever appears necessary. No exceptions. No limits.

In his fine book THE CONSTITUTION OF LIBERTY, economist F.A. Hayek explained, "In Hitler Germany and in Fascist Italy, as well as in Russia, it came to be believed that under the rule of law the state was 'unfree,' a 'prisoner of the law,' and that, in order to act 'justly,' it must be released from the fetters of abstract rules."

America was the opposite, it was founded on the principles of the old common law. This was a complex system of thought based on the two rules taught by all major religions: (1) Do all you have agreed to do. This was the basis of contract law. (2) Do not encroach on other persons or their property. This was the basis of tort law and some criminal law. These laws were not made up, they were discovered through trial and error, like the laws of physics and biology. They are what works. When they are widely obeyed, life gets better; when they are violated, life gets worse. It's automatic.

A third philosophy, **socialism**, also had a detailed plan of the way the world ought to be. The plan didn't work but it was a guide that was followed to a large extent in many nations including the Union of Soviet Socialist Republics.

Unfortunately, by legitimatizing covetousness, socialism swept the world and buried common law.

Now, with the fall of the Soviet Empire, socialism has been discredited, so — and here come thirteen of the most important words you will ever read — *there is no longer any coherent system of law that is widely known.* Fascism — do whatever appears necessary — stands alone and is winning by default.

Chris, in my next letter I'll show the depravity to which the Romans were led by this "whatever appears necessary" philosophy. Until then remember that Hitler and Mussolini rose to power by promising not war, but prosperity and greatness.

Uncle Eric

"I think Russia is moving toward a form of fascism because of poverty, backwardness, frustration, disappointment, fear and the law of the jungle that increasingly prevails in Russian society."

— *Zbigniew Brzezinski*
former National Security Advisor

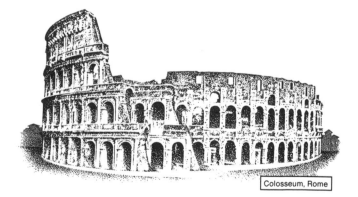

Colosseum, Rome

5

The Roman Lust for Blood

Dear Chris,

By 1994, in the absence of any kind of theoretical guidance, leaders in the former USSR had become like the Germans and Italians in the 1930s. They were reverting to the Roman model, doing whatever appeared necessary.

Were these people crazy or evil? Putting myself in their place, if I had been a socialist who had seen socialism crumble, and if I knew nothing of common law, I might revert to fascism, too. What else is there?

This is why I am afraid that no one can stop the former Soviet Empire from sliding into war and a dark age. If the West could teach them about common law, there would be reason for hope, but the West can't teach what it has forgotten. It is cruising along on the momentum from the work of America's founders, and this momentum may be running out now. Aside from the readers of my book WHATEVER HAPPENED TO JUSTICE?, I doubt there are a thousand people left in the world who understand the connection between common law and economics, and, as far as I know, few of them are in positions of influence. I'm afraid the former USSR will go the way of Rome because it has no other way to go.

Rome gets my vote as the most cruel society ever known. They routinely sent their soldiers — their own flesh and blood — to fight and die in far off wars that had nothing to do with defending their homeland. Their government claimed to have "interests" there, and this was reason enough to go to war. (More about "interests" in a future letter.)

The Romans celebrated murder. In the Colosseum 50,000 would cheer as the government subjected innocent people to unspeakable tortures. The most popular events were those in which family members were forced to kill each other.

This brutality went on not for years, as in the case of the Nazis, or for decades, as in the case of the Soviet socialists, but for centuries. Entire countries were emptied of all their lions, bears and other predators as these animals were sent to fight and feed in amphitheaters all over the Empire.

The Coliseum has been called "the temple of all demons." Roman officials believed the slaughter was essential to keep the crowds happy.

Whatever appears necessary.

On January 25, 1994, Russian officials announced huge new subsidies for farmers and a new system of regulations for energy and natural resources. At the same time they repeated their support for free markets. This is fascism, it is not only cruel, it has no objection to lies or contradictions. Whatever appears necessary.

Since it assumes there is no law higher than the government's law, fascism requires total obedience to the state. It is nationalistic, hyperpatriotic, the ultimate in "my country right or wrong." Militaristic, it glorifies soldiers who are willing to go anywhere and fight anyone.

Fascists love war, to them it is the greatest human adventure. Throughout Hitler's writings and speeches we see references to blood; the red Nazi flag was called the Blood Flag.

On January 26, 1994, Zhirinovsky told reporters he is looking forward to President Clinton and other NATO leaders asking Russia to invade and subdue the war ravaged Caucasus and Islamic areas.

I fear that's the direction the former Soviet Empire is headed and I can see no hope of stopping it. In 1945, common law was still understood to some extent and its principles were available to give the conquered Germans, Italians and Japanese a fresh start down the road to liberty. Today, even America is fast becoming Roman. Juries are instructed to assume there is no law higher than the government's law; justice is whatever lawmakers say it is. With no one to show them the real road to liberty and abundance, the Russians are like the Germans and Italians of the 1930s, looking for a leader to save them, to guide them to greatness, to do whatever appears necessary.

And, it isn't just Russians. By 1994, fascism had begun spreading throughout east Europe. With no coherent system of political thought, each beleaguered ethnic group was becoming fixated on its ancestral homeland. They were looking for a hero to rescue their "Fatherland" from enemies real or imagined. Bigotry and hatred were spreading. Said U.S. NEWS & WORLD REPORT on January 10, 1994, this was leading to "a European disunity of tiny warring homelands, all sacred and all worth dying for."

Let me emphasize, in Russia it wasn't just Zhirinovsky's fascists who were headed down the road to chaos, it was virtually everyone including President Yeltsin and his "reformers." Yeltsin said the historical figure he admired most was Peter the Great. The leading "reform" party in Russia, Russia's Choice, had as its symbol a silhouette of Peter the Great.

Who was Peter? In his attempt to westernize Russia and expand its empire, Czar Peter waged war against neighboring nations. He relentlessly persecuted his domestic opposition, torturing and murdering by the hundreds. A true Roman.

Even the so-called communists adopted fascism. They didn't call it this, but they too now used the "whatever appears necessary" approach. They even allowed private property, a strict taboo under communism.

In his February 24, 1994 State of the Union address, Yeltsin reversed his stand on free-market reforms. On every public issue he called for "a strong state." This included, he said, a willingness to "shoulder the burden of peacemaking in this geographic region" and to regard as a "national cause" the protection of the 25 million Russians living in nearby countries. Clearly he had gone over to the side of the fascists, and had visions of empire.

So, by the end of 1994, Russia had become almost a mirror image of 1930s Germany and Italy, but with the addition of nuclear, chemical and biological weapons. SOVETSKAYA ROSSIYA in Moscow ran an editorial saying the Russian Empire should be rebuilt along the lines of "ancient Rome."[8]

Chris, in my next letter we'll talk about our country's vital interests, Cicero and logic. Until then remember that the essence of Roman law during the Roman Empire was that the government should do whatever appears necessary, no exceptions, no limits. The common law that had been developing during the Roman Republic had been destroyed.

Uncle Eric

---

[8] Quoted in WORLD PRESS REVIEW April 94 p. 13.

6

Logic vs. Interests

Dear Chris,

As explained in my earlier letters, before the Roman Republic became the hated and feared Roman Empire its economy was based on an early form of common law. The premise of this law is that there is a Higher Law than any government's law — the same premise as the Nuremburg Trials. Common law was the attempt to discover and apply this Higher Law.

Roman philosopher Cicero (c.100 B.C.) explained, "For reason did exist, derived from the Nature of the universe, urging men to right conduct and diverting them from wrong-doing, and this reason did not first become Law when it was written down, but when it first came into existence." Of made-up political laws Cicero said, "What of the many deadly, the many pestilential statutes which nations put in force? These no more deserve to be called laws than the rules a band of robbers might pass in their assembly." America's founders studied the writings of Cicero and applied what they learned.

Governments hate the idea of a Higher Law, it limits their power; they work tirelessly to erase our memory of it. They've largely succeeded.

In his 1993 inaugural speech President Clinton declared boldly, "When our vital interests are challenged, or the will and conscience of the international community is defied, we will act, with peaceful diplomacy whenever possible, with force when necessary."

He said vital interests. What's a vital interest?

If you've traveled much abroad you've probably noticed that Americans as individuals are liked and admired but our government is hated and feared. Why? Interests.

The US government contains none of the character or genius that is America. Our government today is Roman. Since 1945, any foreign tyrant who claimed to be pro-US was showered with money, weapons, anything he needed to keep his victims down. The Roman model. Members of the US "sphere of influence" (empire) included the Shah of Iran, Noriega in Panama, Marcos in the Philippines, Batista in Cuba, Diem in Vietnam, Saddam Hussein in Iraq — the list of cutthroats goes on for pages.

It was for interests. There was a day when US troops were expected to fight and die for liberty. Now it's interests. This has been going on for decades — to the point that now no one questions it. Some officials use the term vital interests, and others national interests. Some say strategic interests, and many just say interests.

Nowhere in the Constitution is the word "interests" defined. But we know where it came from. The Roman Senate declared that Emperor Vespasian "shall have the right . . . to do whatever he deems to serve the interests of the state."

Interests, because it is undefined, can mean anything. So, in actual practice interests means carte blanche to do anything to anyone. That's the power that was given to Emperor Vespasian, and it's become the power that is sought by most politically involved persons in the United States today.

We can see in Cicero's remark that the early Roman common law contained elements of Aristotelian logic. Under the Empire this logic was destroyed and replaced by the assumption that laws can be made up according to the rule, whatever appears necessary. Without a moral compass, the law became a destroyer. To Roman civilization, it brought a deluge of economic sabotage: trade restrictions, crushing taxes, inflation, price controls and welfare programs. The eventual result was poverty, chaos, endless war and then feudalism and that horrible five-century depression called the Dark Ages.

Not until the year 1140 did Bolognese jurist Gratian write his DECRETUM which restored some logic to European law. Thus began the grand climb upward to the American Revolution and the liberty and free markets that made our present civilization possible.

But lawmakers have always hated lawyers and judges who demand logic in the law. In the 1930s Great Depression lawmakers in most nations again finally succeeded in removing the last vestiges of logic, and this resurrected the Roman model, which is now called fascism. Fascism says government should do whatever appears necessary to serve its interests.

World War II exposed the brutality of fascism. But those who saw it are old now and the young have little memory of it. The Roman model is coming back strong, especially in its birthplace Europe.

Fascism assumes lawmakers have the right to intervene anywhere and control anything. In 1994, Germany's Ministry of Agriculture drafted a law requiring dog owners to spend two hours of "quality time" daily with their dogs. Don't laugh, it's a symptom of the Roman disease that is again sweeping the world.

Chris, in my next letter I'll talk about the Roman psychology that has become so much a part of today's world. Until then remember that the essence of Roman law is that there is no law higher than the government's law, and that the government should do whatever appears necessary to serve its interests.

Uncle Eric

7

Listen to the Music

Dear Chris,

One of the best things you can do for your business, career and investments is watch a few movies about the Roman Empire. Rarely are these films historically accurate, but they depict the legend that politicians believe and copy. Watch the 1964 film "The Fall of the Roman Empire" starring Alec Guinness. It's entertaining and the first hour reveals much about the thinking that is now popular in the former USSR, as well as in NATO, the UN and Washington.

Very important: as you watch the movie, note the emotions stirred by the film's martial music. These feelings are no small part of what has been happening in the 20th century, and what is likely to come again, perhaps soon.

Deeply ingrained in European culture, the Roman disease resurfaces every few decades to kill thousands. History repeats. The French national anthem exhorts the French to "drench our fields with the impure blood" of the "ferocious foreign invaders who have come to slit the throats of our sons."

The dream of empire inherited from Rome is one of the key reasons Yugoslavia exploded in war, and why I'm convinced the rest of east Europe and the former USSR will, too. I call this area Chaostan — (pronounced chaos-tan) the land of chaos — because I'm afraid it is headed for what will someday be called the Great Chaos. When a civilization has no common law, its only alternatives are tyranny or chaos. Now that the brutal Soviet government is gone, the lid is off the pressure cooker and the explosion has begun. So far we've seen war in Armenia, Azerbaijan, Tajikistan, Moldova, South Ossetia, Chechnya, Georgia, Iraq and Kuwait, and I fear a lot more is coming.

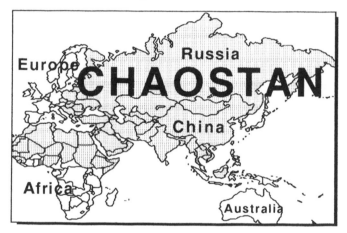

Chaostan, which means the land of chaos, is roughly the area from the Arctic Ocean to the Indian Ocean and Germany to the Pacific, plus north Africa. This vast area — a third of all the land on earth — is inhabited by hundreds of clans, nationalities and ethnic groups who have fought each other for thousands of years. These people have little or no heritage of anything resembling the principles of Common Law.

Until 1990, the bloodshed was kept in check by the tyranny of the Soviet government and the Cold War balances of power. Now the Soviet government is gone and the Cold War has ended. The lid is off the pressure cooker and the explosion has begun. We've already seen outbreaks of fighting in Yugoslavia, Somalia, Iraq and Kuwait, Armenia, Azerbaijan, Tajikistan, Ossetia, Georgia and Moldova, and more is surely coming.

It appears the fall of the Soviet Empire is copying the fall of the Roman Empire, leading to the same end, a dark age of poverty and war.

Each of these dozens of ethnic groups believes they have a right to the lands once controlled by their former empire when that empire was at its zenith. Bulgarians, for instance, believe that since the Bulgarian Empire in the 10th century extended all the way to include Albania, then all this land is theirs by right. This land includes Kosovo, which Serbs claim because it was theirs in the 14th century.

Worse, European and Asian memories are hopelessly long, there are no bygones. In the Bosnian town of Pale, Serb troops wear patches commemorating the Battle of Kosovo in 1389. That was when Moslems defeated Serbs and gained control of the Balkans for 500 years.

The love of the Roman model is so strong in Europe that an entire nation, Romania, is named after Rome. Romania's inhabitants claim direct descent from Emperor Trajan's legions.

In 1994, I visited British and French areas of the Caribbean. It's a great way to get a feel for the effects of the Roman disease. On St. Marten Island, I stood in the hilltop Fort St. Louis where the British and French fought each other in the 1700s. These people boarded small, leaky wooden boats and sailed 4,000 miles of treacherous ocean to that remote dot of land, to climb that hill and kill each other. That's the Roman model — blood, conquest, empire, the glory of war.

The Roman model is becoming increasingly popular. The leader of one of the parties that won the 1994 Italian elections called Mussolini "the greatest statesman of the century."

President Habyarimana of Rwanda, who was killed in a plane crash that year, had been referred to by his soldiers as "Caesar."

In his book THE LAST THRUST SOUTHWARD, Russian fascist Vladimir Zhirinovsky advocated a political philosophy and military strategy taken straight from the pages of Hitler, Mussolini and the Roman emperors. This is the stuff world wars are made of. Wrote Zhirinovsky:

> "Civilization has always started from the south. But since there were too many people in the south they gradually advanced toward the north. People never realized that they were abandoning the better places. Thus my idea of the last thrust.
>
> "It should be done like shock therapy, unexpectedly, quickly and efficiently. We'll acquire the four-axis platform: Relying on the Arctic Ocean in the north; the Pacific Ocean in the east; the Atlantic Ocean through the Black, Mediterranean and Baltic Seas; and finally in the south, on the Indian Ocean, we shall get quiet neighbors.
>
> "Such are the historical realities; a merger of different nations as a result of the economy, the dominance of the Russian language, the Russian ruble, the dominant place of the Russian army as the most combat capable. Stability in the entire region. ... America will rest in peace because this will mean an end to wars in this region of the world — no Red threat, no Muslim or Turk threats, no Islamic threat.
>
> "It has always been a dream of mine — to see Russian soldiers wash their army boots in the warm water of the Indian Ocean and change into summer uniforms forever . . . We will build sanatoriums, spas, youth camps on the vast expanses of the south for the people from the industrial north to take a rest there. Let the Muslims stick to their customs and traditions in places where they live in large numbers. ...
>
> "All these things will become possible if we make this thrust to the south. We need it badly. It is the medicine that everyone has to take."

Zhirinovsky may or may not achieve his dream. He may vanish and be forgotten. What will be important is that he and his fascist ideas are supported by millions. If he goes, we can expect someone of like mind to take his place.

Chris, in my next letter I'll tell you what I learned about the Roman disease during my trip to England. Until then remember how much the world loves the Roman model, and how Roman ideas stir the emotions.

Uncle Eric

Why Do They Do It?

Sometimes it seems the US government never turns down an invitation to a war. Why? Here's a possible explanation.

The Bill of Rights stops at the border. Inside the US, the Bill of Rights protects us against the government's use of arbitrary power. But beyond the borders, US officials can do anything they want.

Why do they do it? Because it's exhilarating. I vividly remember when I was a young man in the Air Force during the 1960s, standing in the door of the AC-47 "Dragonship" listening to the roar of the guns and watching the column of fire pour down on the target. The Ride of the Valkyries! I felt invincible and all-powerful. I'm older now and embarrassed to admit I was thrilled by it, but I was.

Imagine what it must be like to command the entire US military. Could any human do it without having his judgement hopelessly corrupted? Who could resist the temptation to be a crusader meddling in the affairs of other nations?

This is one reason America's founders wanted us to rely on a "well regulated militia" like that of Switzerland — thoroughly capable of protecting the country but neither trained or equipped to fight abroad.

"Never was so much false arithmetic employed on any subject, as that which has been employed to persuade nations that it is in their interest to go to war."
— Thomas Jefferson, 1781

8

The Return of Feudalism

Dear Chris,

History may not repeat exactly but it does repeat, and it gives guidance. The fundamental reason history repeats is that governments cling to the Roman model and endlessly repeat Roman blunders, both in the economy and in foreign policy.

The collapse of the Soviet Empire has been proceeding much like the collapse of the Roman Empire — one of the great catastrophes of human history. This leads me to fear that we may be facing a new world war in east Europe, Asia and north Africa, the area I call Chaostan.

Fighting first broke out along the Soviet Empire's fringes — Iraq, Yugoslavia, Somalia, Moldova, Georgia, Azerbaijan, Armenia, Yemen and Tajikistan. So, in 1993 I spent three weeks doing research in England which was the most distant fringe of the old Roman Empire and the area where the collapse of Roman civilization was first felt. I visited five old Roman cities — London, Bath, York, Caerphilly and Canterbury — to see how closely events there presaged events now.

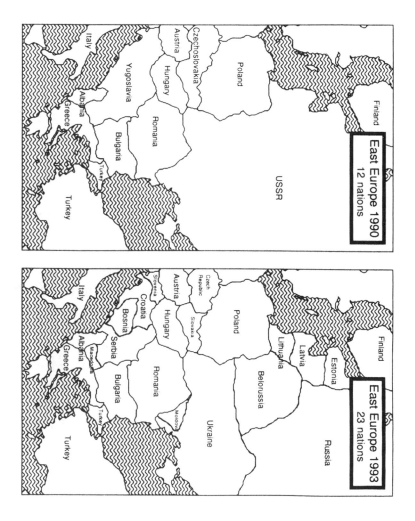

Chris, it was fascinating. The bottom line is that, so far, events in and around the former Soviet Empire today have been virtual carbon copies of events in England fifteen centuries ago, although the technology now is more advanced and the rate of change much faster. Events that took decades then take only months or weeks now.

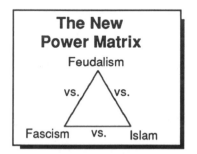

The power matrix of the past 50 years was two-sided, Soviet socialism vs. US democracy. The new matrix is three-sided, feudalism vs. fascism vs. Islam. Presently feudalism is winning[9] but fascism and Islam are coming on strong.[10] Nothing will affect our investments more.

Like the hundreds of ethnic groups in the former USSR, the various tribes of the Roman Empire had no common law of their own. They had only the law imposed on them from above by Rome (in the USSR law was imposed by the Kremlin). When the Romans left England, law and order left with them. The tribes split into tiny new nations and began warring with each other, as is happening now in the old Soviet Empire.

Like the USSR, Rome was a major military power. But its thirst for military goods was puny compared to that of the medieval warlords. These tyrants were voracious consumers of armor, weapons and fortifications. To pay for it all,

---

[9] See Richard Maybury's EARLY WARNING REPORT July, 1993, published by Henry-Madison Research, Box 1616-AR, Rocklin, CA.

[10] The war with Islam is explained in THE NEXT WORLD WAR HAS BEGUN, a special report by Richard Maybury, published by Henry-Madison Research.

the warlords taxed their people into a kind of slavery called **serfdom**.

Someday, Chris, be sure to visit the town of Caerphilly in Wales. The Roman fort there was small, enclosing perhaps one acre and resembling a US frontier cavalry fort with low, thin wooden walls. The medieval castle that replaced it will leave you awestruck, it must be seen to be believed. With its moat and outlying fortifications it covers at least 12 acres. The stone walls are ten feet thick and fifty feet high. Even with today's weapons this citadel would not be easy to conquer. The people who built it were clearly terrified of their neighbors.

Caerphilly Castle in Wales
To grasp the awesome size of the castle, note the truck in the castle courtyard. (Book's cover photo is Caerphilly Castle.)

Chris, now that you understand what happened after the fall of Rome, how serious do you think the chaos will become in the former USSR?

My guess is that Chaostan is sliding into a dark age.

If the thought of a dark age in Chaostan doesn't make the hair on the back of your neck stand up, you might not fully understand what a dark age is. Let me explain.

Visualize an ancient Roman city. From the air it would have been almost indistinguishable from a city today. The buildings, some up to five stories high, were brick, stone, concrete and marble with tile roofs. The streets were straight and paved.

Inside the buildings you would have found central heating, plumbing, baths, and walls plastered and painted. You'd walk on beautiful mosaic tile floors and peer out glass windows. In the center of the city you'd see theaters, forums and amphitheaters, buildings large even by today's standards.

The Roman highway system is legendary. It made a swift pony express mail system possible, and fostered trade that supplied finished goods and raw materials from England to the Red Sea, an expanse of 2500 miles.

This was an extensive, advanced civilization well supplied with food by a system of plantations called **latifundia**. Factories mass-produced pottery and metalwork. But then ...

The Empire splintered into these tiny independent states ruled by tinpot dictators. Bloodshed and poverty spread. Death by the sword and starvation became common as most of what the Romans had built was destroyed. We see this repeated nightly now in television newscasts about Yugoslavia, Armenia, Somalia, Chechnya and a great many other places.

The destruction of Roman civilization was so complete it is hard for the imagination to grasp. In England, for the two hundred years after 400 A.D., the record is almost blank, we do not know exactly what happened. But when history picks up again around 600 A.D., here is what we find.

London had been one of the largest, most important cities of the Roman Empire. By 600 A.D. so little of it remained that historians today are unable to prove it existed at all during that 200 year period.

We know Canterbury was entirely destroyed and abandoned.

The beautiful resort city of Bath was flattened as if it had been hit by an atomic bomb. An 8th century poem about Bath was called "The Ruin." By the end of the Middle Ages the site had reverted to woodland so completely that there was no sign a city had ever been there. Not a brick, not a statue, nothing remained above ground. An archaeologist discovered remains of the Roman city accidentally when digging there in 1755.

This chaos, which started on the fringes of the Empire, spread until it had engulfed all of Europe and most of the Mediterranean world. The brick and stone Roman cities were completely demolished, as has been happening in town after town in Yugoslavia today.

Note this. Of all the *hundreds* of Roman cities and towns, *not one* survived the barbarism intact. The most we can see today are a few bits and pieces of fortress walls and ruined buildings. The theater at Orange in France, the bridge across the Tagus in Spain, the baths at Trier in Germany, the Deir tomb in Saudi Arabia and the remains of the city of Timgad in Algeria are some of the most heart-rending examples of the total destruction of this vast civilization.

A June 6, 1993 Associated Press story about a new Serb offensive in Bosnia said 40 Moslem villages had "vanished from the face of the earth." Moslems blamed the carnage on

Washington's meddling and called the area "Clinton's grave-yard."

After the Roman civilization was destroyed, the people lost the ability to read and write. They forgot math, science and engineering, and returned to the primitive living conditions of a thousand years earlier.

In England they became near-savages living barely above the stone age. With their wonderful cities destroyed, they reverted to one-room huts of sticks and mud; no sanitation, an incessant shortage of food, and little knowledge of the outside world. Their lives were all toil, filth, disease, crushing taxes and war, endless war.

They stayed that way achieving little progress for 950 years until the black plague killed off the feudal lords in 1350.

What was the root cause of it all? The Romans had fallen prey to socialism. This cancerous system of mushrooming welfare, high taxes, trade restrictions and inflation destroyed the Roman system of common law and demolished the currency and the economy. By 400 A.D. the troops were no longer well paid and, as in the former Union of Soviet Socialist Republics today, some units went renegade.

When the Romans withdrew, the local people were left with no law and no military defense unless they could hire one of these renegade Roman units, as is happening in parts of the old USSR now. Commanders of the renegade units became local dictators, as in the USSR today.

The roads fell into disrepair. Long distance trade and communication ceased. And, as is happening now in the former USSR, supplies of raw materials from distant lands began to dry up. Mass production ended and towns started preying on each other. Each latifundium became a separate nation struggling to survive in isolation from the rest of the world. Each had to build its own castle and army. Taxes, taxes and more taxes.

500 B.C.

Before Roman civilization came to Britain the inhabitants lived in primitive log huts with dirt floors, no sanitation and no windows.

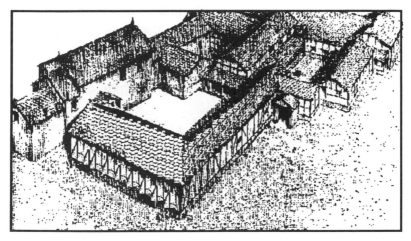

200 A.D. *Roman civilization brought large tile roofed buildings with mosaic floors, plumbing, baths, glass windows and central heating.*

500 A.D.

Then the Roman government's taxes, inflation, regulations and wars demolished the economy. The Dark Ages began, and the inhabitants were reduced to living as they had a thousand years before.

In our school books we are taught that the Roman Empire fell because it had become militarily weak and was overrun by tribes of barbarians. This is a half-truth. In most areas, civilization had already been destroyed by socialism; the people were well down the road to barbarism themselves long before the arrival of the foreign tribes.

In some cases these foreign tribes did not need to fight their way in, they were *welcomed* as rescuers.

That's a dark age, and I fear this is what is coming all across the former Soviet Empire and surrounding areas — a third of all the land on earth. It will not be the liberty and free markets that United States officials and the mainstream press speak of, but economic chaos, persecutions, death and destruction.

You might be questioning my pessimism. How can I be so certain you might ask?

Because they have no model[11] to guide them. They have nothing resembling common law. The wars in Yugoslavia, Somalia, Armenia, Azerbaijan, Yemen, Moldova, Iraq and Tajikistan are only the beginning.

In China, too, feudalism is beginning to rear its ugly head. The central government's power is slipping away as farms and factories come under total control of local strongmen. In one Chinese steel mill in 1993 the managers decided that workers must work 365 days per year. Farmers in Sichuan province rioted over new taxes levied by local officials.

This new feudalism will be like that of a thousand years ago except that the barbarians then did not have tanks, planes

---

[11] See explanation of "Uncle Eric's" Model beginning on page 6 of this book.

and guided missiles, not to mention nuclear, chemical and biological weapons.

Greatly aggravating all this is the fact that, locked behind the Iron Curtain for a half-century, east Europe is stuck in a time warp. Over there it's still 1939, crazy nationalists are gaining influence fast. In 1993 the TORONTO STAR reported that the leader of the Hungarian Path Movement, Istvan Csurka, said Hungary is being damaged by "Jews and the dilution of Hungarian genes" and needs more "lebensraum" (living space). This is straight from the pages of Hitler's MEIN KAMPF. Csurka has followers among Hungarians living in neighboring countries who want to split off and unite with Hungary. Hungary is (was?) regarded as one of the more stable, forward-looking east European nations.

I'm afraid a bloody free-for-all across all Chaostan is now as certain as anything in human affairs can be.

Chris, in my next letter I'll write about the importance of straight lines. Until then remember that an advanced civilization is made possible by the principles of common law. When those principles are not widely obeyed, the consequence can be a dark age.

Uncle Eric

What We've Lost

Chris, the collapse of Roman civilization is still costing us today. Think about what we've lost.

The Roman grist mill near Arles, in what is today France, was amazing. With 16 water wheels operating in tandem, and a complex system of gears and grinders, it could produce enough flour for a population of 80,000. This kind of engineering sophistication leads me to believe Roman civilization was on the brink of the industrial revolution 15 centuries before this revolution finally happened.

At just the point where Roman science and technology had reached the take-off point, Roman civilization began sliding backward. So, today we are 15 centuries behind where we should be.

It's probably not an exaggeration to say that by now we would have had cures for all diseases, colonies throughout the solar system, no poverty, greatly extended lifespans, you name it. I'd love to have the ability to visit any historical site or vacation paradise anywhere on earth as easily as I visit the neighboring town today, and I'm sure it would have been possible.

But we aren't there yet, and won't be for a long time, because the advance of civilization was reversed for so long by the collapse of Roman civilization. It was probably the biggest set back in all history.

9

Straight Lines

Dear Chris,

Look at a globe. Where do you see straight lines? Therein lies a tale important for understanding our world today.

The Romans were great road builders. Wherever they subdued other people and captured their victims' homeland, the Romans would build fine, paved roads connecting their forts and towns. In England today whenever you find yourself driving on a long, straight road it's probably an old Roman road.

The psychological effect of these roads on the conquered people must have been profound. Put yourself in their place. One day these strangers, from a distant place you've never heard of, suddenly appear in your community. They begin collecting taxes and ruthlessly slaughtering anyone who resists. You and your family try to mount a defense but they have weapons and tactics you've never seen before, and you are easily beaten.

Then they build their roads, their long, straight roads, for purposes you cannot imagine. All you know about these roads is that one day you see the road builders on the horizon laying their road in the direction of your property. Their long, straight road.

Steadily laying pavement, they move toward you destroying anything that gets in their way. Trees, rocks, homes, churches, you name it, if it is in the way of the road, it goes. When finished, the long, straight road stretches from as far as you can see in one direction to as far as you can see in the other.

It cuts right through your back yard, and for the rest of your life you are reminded every day when you look out your window that you do not control your property or your life.

The Roman road is not just for transportation, it's a message. It is the Romans saying, we don't respect you, we don't care about you, we own you and we can do anything we please including kill you; don't make us angry.

Now look back at the globe. Where do you see the straight lines?

These are the borders of nations that were created not by the native people who lived there but by Europeans. Following the Roman model, the Europeans fanned out across the globe conquering other civilizations. Dividing the land among themselves, they drew the borders in ways convenient to them, that is, in long straight lines.

Ordinarily humans use natural boundaries to separate cultures. Rivers and mountain ranges are the most common.

The Europeans drew their borders cutting right across the natural borders of the native people. In many cases, clans who had never done anything to provoke the Europeans would suddenly find a line drawn right through their homeland with part of their clan living in one country and part in another—like the Berlin Wall dividing East and West Germany. The Berlin Wall was Roman.

In most cases where you see straight borders you are looking at areas where Europeans, following the Roman model, attacked and conquered the native people and divided up the land. Egypt, for instance, was taken by French and British, Libya by Italians, Algeria by French, and Morocco by French and Spanish. North America was conquered by British, French and Spanish. In all these cases, the Europeans were copying the Romans, building empires.

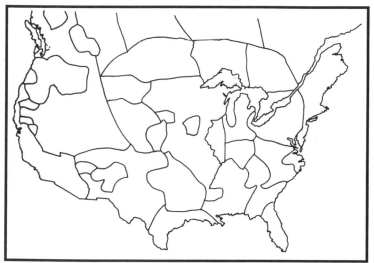

Native American Homelands

Indian nations did not have formal borders. The map above approximates tribal homelands before European impact. Contrast the map above to the one below.

North Africa / Mid-east Map
*In the US most of the native peoples were killed. In Asia and Africa
they were not, and today they still live with the artificial borders. This
is one of the main causes of the wars erupting in those parts of the world.*

We see most of these long, straight borders in Central
Asia, Africa, the Mideast, Australia and North America.
These are the places where the Europeans, following the
Roman example, conquered the natives and divided up the
land for their own purposes.

Often they built railroads, long, straight railroads, cutting right across the land of the original owners. Sometimes
the owners would resist, as when American Indians would
attack trains, but usually it was to no avail.

Fascinating isn't it, that in a very real way the American
Indians were conquered by Rome.

Today, many of the new wars that have broken out in
and around the former Soviet Empire are the result of the
long, straight borders. Following the Roman model, the
Moscow regime had conquered the native people and sent in
Russians to colonize and "administer" these people. Now

that the Moscow regime is weak, these conquered peoples have been declaring independence. But what to do about the borders? There is very little agreement about which pieces of land should be in which countries, and wars are breaking out in many areas.

Officially the old USSR contained 126 nationalities. That is, it contained 125 nationalities who were conquered by the Russians. The Russians drew the borders. Now that the Soviet Empire is breaking up, the National Academy of Sciences has calculated there are at least 76 cases of borders in dispute.

I fear little of this is understood in Washington D.C. because most of our politicians and bureaucrats *believe in the Roman model!* They think it's a good thing to have a strong central government that owns and controls everything and everybody, so the politicians and bureaucrats are incapable of understanding what's gone wrong. They know nothing of common law. I'm afraid many think the fighting is due to the splintering of Moscow's Empire so the solution is to recreate a new strong central government — to strengthen the Roman model.

What's the real solution? I don't believe there is one. Few of these nationalities have anything resembling the principles of common law, so they have no way to sort out their differences or to live together in peace. Their natural condition since the beginning of history has been war, and I think they are returning to this condition.

Chris, in my next letter I'll talk about the **Byzantine Empire**. Until then remember that in most cases a straight border is an unnatural border and a likely cause of war. It is a sign of the Roman disease.

Uncle Eric

10

The Byzantine Empire

Dear Chris,

Thanks, I'm glad these stories about Rome and its lessons for us today are raising so many questions in your mind. For a fascinating picture of the Roman Empire and the Roman psychology that is behind the new wars today, get the video "Roman City."[12]

Although the Roman Empire in Europe finally collapsed around 500 A.D., the eastern portion, centered in what is today Turkey, continued for another thousand years. Called the Byzantine Empire, it was thoroughly Roman, meaning it was loaded with high taxes, regulations, welfare programs and a monstrous bureaucracy, like Washington D.C., that controlled every facet of economic life. This is where we get the term Byzantine, meaning a hopelessly complex and devious government riddled with corruption and intrigue.

In 528 A.D., Byzantine emperor Justinian had tried to simplify Roman law. It worked, partly, condensing the Roman tangle into a "mere" 4,652 laws. (You might remember from our earlier correspondence that the United States

---

[12] Available from PBS Video. Phone 1-800-328-7271.

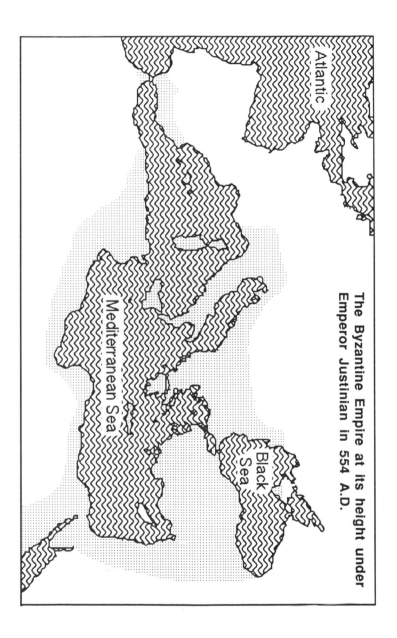

The Byzantine Empire at its height under Emperor Justinian in 554 A.D.

Atlantic

Mediterranean Sea

Black Sea

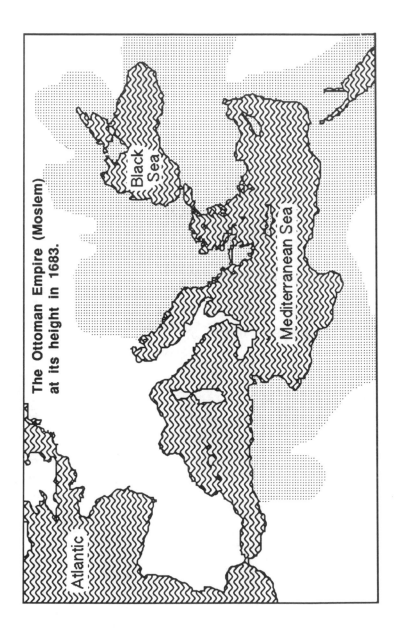

The Ottoman Empire (Moslem) at its height in 1683.

Black Sea

Mediterranean Sea

Atlantic

today has hundreds of thousands of federal, state, and local law.) These became the foundation of the Byzantine government and eventually of law across most of Europe. The principle exceptions were England and Ireland that, protected by the ocean, were freer to develop their own common law systems.

As explained in my previous letters, this Roman law was later interpreted to mean there is no law higher than the government's law, justice is whatever lawmakers say it is. This is the premise of all law today, and it led to the rise of fascism and World War II. It is now again sparking the wars that are spreading across Chaostan. Under that kind of law, everyone is forced to fight for control of the government, for to be without this control is to be a sheep among wolves.

With all its laws, taxes and bureaucracy, how did the Byzantine Empire survive when the rest of the Roman Empire couldn't? The capital was Constantinople (now Istanbul). Located on the Bosporus Strait, which is only 1800 feet wide, this tiny dot of land was the crossroads — or more accurately the chokepoint — for trade between Europe and the Orient. It was and still is one of the most profitable and strategic spots on earth. The huge revenues garnered from it kept the Byzantine Empire alive.

Christianity was the official religion of the Byzantine Empire. Then, in 1054, church officials in Constantinople and Rome quarreled, and excommunicated each other. This split Christianity, giving us the Roman Catholic church in the West and the Eastern Orthodox church in the East.

The Byzantines traveled far and wide making converts, and two of the groups they converted to the Eastern Orthodox faith were the Russians and Serbs.

But the Byzantine government continued to grow, and its taxes, regulations and bureaucracy finally brought the same fate as in Rome. In 1453, the weakened Byzantine civilization was overrun and conquered by the Ottoman Turks, who were Moslem.

An interesting sidelight here is that in conquering the Mediterranean world, Moslems took many cities not by force but by simply telling the inhabitants that if they became Moslems their backbreaking taxes would be cut. Many cities welcomed Moslems as saviors.

With Turkey converted to Islam, this left Russians and Serbs on the front lines of the Christian world against the Islamic world. Russians and Serbs became allies and fought a series of wars against the Turks.

The most disputed territories were those around the Black Sea, including Crimea, and the Balkans. The Moslems had colonized these areas, and the Russians and Serbs wanted to push them out. Also, Russians wanted free access to the Black Sea, Mediterranean and Atlantic, but the Turks had Istanbul.

The lead troops of the Russians were the Cossacks. Fiercely Christian, Cossack tribes were and still are mortal enemies of Moslems.

Now that the Soviet government is gone, the lid is off the pressure cooker and the ancient Moslem vs. Christian feud has revived. In Bosnia, it takes the form of Serbs versus Moslems. In Tajikistan it's Russians versus Moslems. In the Caucasus mountains it's Cossacks vs. Moslems. In Georgia it's Georgians vs. Moslems.

This is all the same feud, Christians vs. Moslems, a thirteen-century vendetta left over from the days of the Byzantine Empire.

Part of what's happening over there is a revival of "The Eastern Question." Russians wanted to take Istanbul in order to guarantee their access to the Mediterranean, so the British and other rivals of Russia sided with the Turks to keep the Russians bottled up. One of the many wars growing out of the Eastern Question was the 1853 Crimean War. At some point, I fear the wars between Christians and Moslems in the Black Sea area will again lead to an attempt by Russians to take Istanbul.

The Bosporus is one of the most fought-over pieces of real estate on earth.

Most Dangerous Place On Earth

The Balkans are Slovenia, Croatia, Serbia, Bosnia, Macedonia, Albania, Greece, Kosovo, Montenegro, Bulgaria, Romania and the European part of Turkey. This is where some of the most bloody wars between Christians and Moslems have been fought.

What makes all this so much more dangerous and likely to lead to a massive war is that 25 million Russians live outside Russia in the homelands of the people who were once conquered by them at the time of the USSR's breakup. Russians were 23% of the population of Moslem Chechen-Ingustia, 30% of Moslem North Ossetia, 43% of Moslem Tatarstan, and so on for vast areas of the former USSR. These Russians are hated and now persecuted, and the Moscow regime has promised to protect them; it can't handle 25 million refugees pouring into Mother Russia. On June 21, 1994, the Russian parliament voted to send another 3,000 "peacemaking" troops into the former Soviet republic of Georgia.

This two-headed eagle is from a Byzantine manuscript. Watch for it to appear on battle flags in the former USSR.

How can all this not lead to a continent-wide war? How can it not have a dramatic effect on our businesses, careers and investments?

Chris, watch for the two-headed eagle[13], it's a good leading indicator of growing tensions between Christians and Moslems in the Balkans and Black Sea area. This bird was the sign of the Byzantine Empire. Looking both east and west, it symbolized control of the Bosporus. After the Byzantine Empire was overrun by the

---

[13] In western Europe, the two-headed eagle signifies the Hapsburg Empire.

Moslem Turks, Russians assumed leadership of the Christian world against the Moslem world. They adopted the Byzantine coronation ceremony for their czars and the two-headed eagle as their national symbol. Now Russian nationalists are reviving this symbol.

The Bosporus has been fought over so many times that it may be the site of more strategic battles than any other in the world. The more we see that two-headed eagle, the closer we may be to another world-class shoot-out between Christians and Moslems in Chaostan.

Chris, I am forever amazed at how events on the other side of the world a thousand years ago affect us and our money more than do events in our hometowns today. The Roman Empire may be gone but the Roman disease is still killing and impoverishing us by the millions.

In my next letter I'll summarize the important points we've covered in this set of letters. Until then remember that the history we are now seeing unfold in Chaostan is new only in the sense that the rate of change is faster and the weapons are more deadly.

Uncle Eric

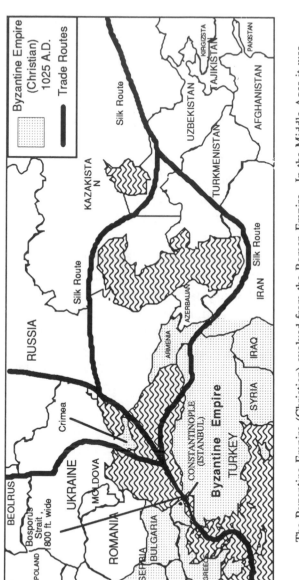

Maps show national boundaries today.

Byzantine Empire
(Christian)
1025 A.D.

Trade Routes

POLAND
BEOLRUS
Bosporus
Strait,
800 ft. wide

RUSSIA

UKRAINE
MOLDOVA
Crimea

KAZAKISTAN

ROMANIA
SERBIA
BULGARIA
GREECE

Byzantine Empire
CONSTANTINOPLE
(ISTANBUL)
TURKEY

Silk Route

ARMENIA
AZERBALIAN

IRAQ
SYRIA
IRAN   Silk Route

Silk Route

UZBEKISTAN
KIRGIZSTAN
TAJIKISTAN
PAKISTAN

TURKMENISTAN

AFGHANISTAN

The Byzantine Empire (Christian) evolved from the Roman Empire. In the Middle Ages it was conquered and replaced by the Ottoman Empire (Moslem). Bloodshed in the Balkans, Armenia, Azerbaijan and other areas shows that the hatreds remain intense.

Note: Turkey today is Moslem. This is a holdover from the Ottoman Empire.

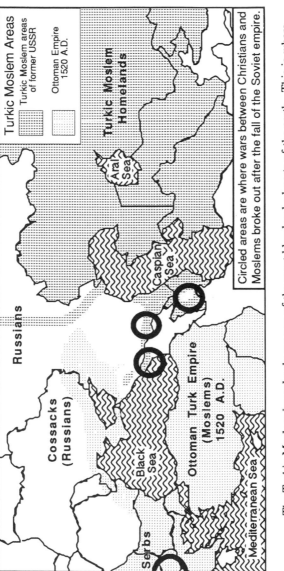

The Turkic Moslem homelands are one of the most bloodsoaked parts of the earth. This is where the Christian and Moslem worlds have collided for more than a thousand years. In the early 1990s, after the fall of the Soviet Empire, the ancient hatreds and rivalries were set loose once again.

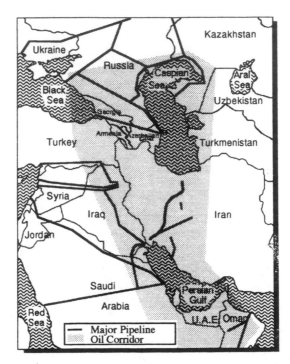

The oil corridor accounts for 40% of the world's daily oil production and has 70% of the world's proven oil reserves.

It also contains thousands of tons of nuclear, chemcial and biological weapons, and is at the center of one of the world's oldest and most virulent feuds. This feud is the Moslem vs. Christian vendetta that stretches back to the days of the Byzantine Empire.

All the Persian Gulf countries are Moslem. So, most of the world's oil is beneath the homelands of Moslems.

Pipelines are easy to sabotage and nearly impossible to guard.

Bear in mind that millions of Moslems hate the West, and with good reason. Since the year 1500 there has rarely been any five year period in which European troops have not been under arms on Moslem soil. The Roman disease.

Some Moslem rulers make a show of being friendly to the West — they want the US government's military protection—but that's probably all it is, a show. The Saudis and Kuwaitis both participated in the oil embargoes against the West, and when the chips are down they can be expected to do so again.

Oil troubles shook the economy and investment markets in 1973, 1979 and 1990, and it looks like there's a lot more coming.

In June, 1994, in what could turn out to be the biggest mistake of the 20th century, the UN sent 1800 *Turkish* troops into the Balkans. "Turkey could naturally not stand by and watch the massacre in Bosnia, with which it has cultural and historical ties," said the Turkish prime minister. If you were a Serb or Russian, how would you take this? Is the UN *trying* to provoke a world war?

"Pentagon threat-assessment officer Major Ralph Peters believes intelligence officers must set aside their preoccupation with numbers and weaponry. Instead, he says, they must start reading books that explain human behavior and regional history."

— *ST. LOUIS POST-DISPATCH*

11

Summary

Dear Chris,

This letter will be short, just a brief summary of what we've covered. Seven points:

1. History can seem like a meaningless collection of names and dates if we do not have a model of how the world works to help us understand it and learn its lessons. The model helps us see what is important and what is not.

2. History repeats—mostly because governments keep repeating the mistakes made by the Roman government. They do this because so many people believe in the Roman model. They look back on the Pax Romana as the good old days and try to recreate it.

3. The Roman model is fascism. Its one and only fundamental principle is that powerholders should do whatever appears necessary, no exceptions and no limits.

4.   During the age of the Roman Republic, which was roughly 500 B.C. to the year 0, Roman civilization grew up and flourished under an early form of common law. This law was then abandoned in favor of arbitrary political law, which eventually became the basis of most law today. Rome's political law was, in my opinion, the root cause of its fall and of the subsequent Dark Ages in Europe.

5.   Roman ideas and symbols are everywhere in our civilization today. They also have great influence in the former Soviet Empire.

6.   Europe has been the source of history's worst wars, including the two world wars, because Europeans have embraced the Roman model and tried to conquer most of the world.

7.   I call the Roman model the Roman disease because of all the bloodshed and poverty it has caused. The Roman disease assumes political power is a good thing.

Chris, regarding your investments, be aware at all times that it looks like the world has entered a period of major upheaval on par with the greatest events in history. The fall of the Soviet Empire promises to be as earthshaking as the fall of the Roman Empire, or the two world wars, the Crusades, the Industrial Revolution, you name it. We can't know what's coming, so stay flexible. Forget about long-term planning, be ready to make changes on a day-to-day basis. Don't get into anything you can't get out of fast. This can be a time of great opportunity for those who are adaptable.

I know you are interested in other books you can read about the conflict between liberty and the Roman disease, and the effects of this conflict on our world today as the Soviet Empire disintegrates. But I don't know of any.

Fortunately, however, there are thousands of books about the Roman Empire and European history. Almost any of these will give you important data. Now that you've read these letters about ancient Rome, and my previous sets of letters about economics and law, you have the ability to extract the information that is important, and ignore that which is not.

Reading other books makes this process even easier, especially Frederick Bastiat's THE LAW, Henry Grady Weaver's MAINSPRING OF HUMAN PROGRESS, Rose Wilder Lane's DISCOVERY OF FREEDOM, and Henry Hazlitt's ECONOMICS IN ONE LESSON. Also, Chris, now that you have both sides of the story about the ancient battle between liberty and power, you are armed with the knowledge you need to read and benefit from books written by authors who may not believe in liberty or free markets. Read the books to glean *facts* about events that actually happened, and *supply your own analysis and interpretation.*

Chris, this I'm sure of — America's present government cannot be saved or reformed, it's much too big and powerful and much too corrupt. It is headed for the same fate as the Soviet government. Maybe not in the next three or four years but, my guess is, in the next ten or twenty. We'll wake up one day, turn on our radios and learn that the US government has disappeared, gone out of business as the Soviet government did in 1991.

This could be our great opportunity, a chance to make a fresh start.

The Roman system does not work, it always leads to crushing taxes, war, inflation, business failures, unemployment and poverty. Because of this I believe America and perhaps most of the world is headed for some kind of major economic catastrophe. Exactly what it will be I don't know. Maybe a hyperinflation, maybe depression or war, maybe a combination of these or something else, it's impossible to say.

America's founders faced a similar crisis. Having studied ancient and contemporary history, they realized the direction England was headed. They watched with horror as the Roman disease began to infect the colonies. To ward off the disease they severed all ties with England. Their efforts resulted in a new nation based on free markets and the two fundamental laws. The founders knew it wouldn't be easy. They risked their lives, fortunes, and sacred honor to provide for themselves and "their posterity — life, liberty and the pursuit of happinesss."

Today's crisis will be grim but it doesn't have to last forever, perhaps no more than two or three years. More importantly, we can come out on the other side headed for a wonderful new civilization. Am I suggesting we turn back the clock and return to the 1700s? On the contrary, I'm suggesting we study our past, learn from it, and either repair the damage or pick up the pieces and begin again — this time avoiding the mistakes America's founders cautioned us against.

Chris, some people will wait for disaster to swallow them up, and others will choose, like America's founders, to passionately fight "for a new nation, conceived in liberty" and dedicated to the two fundamental laws that make an advanced civilization possible.

I can't guarantee your tomorrow. Will it be a new Dark Age like the one that followed the fall of the Roman Empire, or a new Golden Age? The best advice I can offer for the next 90 years is, put as much distance as possible between yourself and all things political, and form friendships and business relationships with persons who believe in liberty and free markets.

Mankind is getting another lesson in what works and what doesn't. Persons who learn the lesson first will profit most.

To head into a Golden Age we must have a rational legal system based on the two fundamental laws. Now is the time to lay the groundwork so spread the word.

Uncle Eric

"The people are paying the unrighteous tribute in hopes that the nation will at length revert to justice. But before that time comes, it is to be feared they will be so accustomed to bondage, as to forget they were ever free."
— *Samuel Adams, 1771*

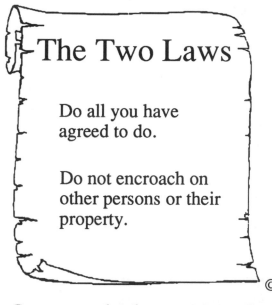

The Two Laws

Do all you have agreed to do.

Do not encroach on other persons or their property.

©

Spread the Word

Comparison of Law Chart
Reprinted from WHATEVER HAPPENED TO JUSTICE? *by Richard J. Maybury*

Natural Law or Common Law was the origin of the original American philosophy, but America has now switched to political law which is a Roman concept.

Scientific Law *(Natural Law or Common Law)*	Political Law *(Legislation)*
Requirements	
Based on fact, logic and the two fundamental laws: (1) do all you have agreed to do, (2) do not encroach on other persons or their property.	Whatever the powerholders decide.
"All men are created equal"—no special exemptions or privileges.*	Whatever the powerholders decide.
Cautious and hesitant in the use of force.	Whatever the powerholders decide.
Characteristics	
Predictable, knowable.	Whimsical.
Evolutionary change. Few reversals.	Frequent revolutionary changes. Many reversals.
Discovered by judges, one case at a time.	Made up by politicians in response to political pressure and "influence."
Highly developed, advanced.	Primitive.
Results	
Tends to neutralize political power.	Gives powerseekers more power.
Creates liberty and security.	Destroys liberty and security.
Makes effective economic calculation possible—spurs creation of wealth and abundance.	Uses force to redistribute wealth. Destroys incentive to produce wealth.
Stable economic environment.	Boom-and-bust cycles.
Enables civilization to advance.	Destroys civilizations.

*Applies to all mentally competent adults, whether acting as individuals or in groups. The problem of children and mentally incompetent adults remains unsolved under both systems.

Please Write "Uncle Eric" With Your Ideas, Questions and Concerns

Watch for future books by Richard J. Maybury. One will be answers to questions from readers. Send your questions or comments to him in care of "Uncle Eric," Bluestocking Press, P.O. Box 1014, Dept. AR, Placerville, CA 95667-1014. All letters become property of Bluestocking Press and may be published in whole or in part without payment to the writer. Please tell us if you want your name kept confidential. Topics can include, but are not limited to economics, government, history and law.

If your letter is published in a future "Uncle Eric" book or used in a future "Uncle Eric" audiocassette tape you will receive a free autographed copy of that book or tape.

Bibliography

- ANCIENT LAW by Sir Henry Sumner Maine, Dorset Press, Great Britain, 1861, 1986.
- ATLAS OF THE ROMAN WORLD by Tim Cornell and John Matthews, Facts on File, Inc., NY, 1990.
- ARE YOU LIBERAL? CONSERVATIVE? OR CONFUSED? by Richard J. Maybury, Bluestocking Press, Placerville, CA, 1995.
- ATLAS OF RUSSIAN HISTORY by Martin Gilbert, Dorset Press, Great Britain, 1972.
- BYZANTIUM by Philip Sherrard, Time-Life Books, NY, 1966.
- CONSTITUTION OF LIBERTY by Friedrich A. Hayek, University of Chicago Press, 1960.
- DECLINE AND FALL OF THE ROMAN EMPIRE by Edward Gibbon, Penguin Books, NY, 1985.
- EVALUATING BOOKS: WHAT WOULD THOMAS JEFFERSON THINK ABOUT THIS? by Richard J. Maybury, Bluestocking Press, Placerville, CA, 1994.
- HISTORY'S TIMELINE by Jean Cooke, Ann Kramer and Theodore Rowland-Entwistle, Crescent Books, NY, 1981.
- HITLER'S GERMAN ENEMIES by Louis L. Snyder, Hippocrene Books, NY, 1990.
- IMPERIAL ROME by Moses Hadas, Time-Life Books, NY, 1965.
- LAW IN AMERICA, A HISTORY, by Bernard Schwartz, McGraw-Hill, NY, 1974.
- LAW, ITS NATURE, FUNCTION AND LIMITS, by Charles G. Howard and Robert S. Summers, Prentice-Hall, Inc., Englewood Cliffs, NJ, 1965.
- LIFE AND SELECTED WRITINGS OF THOMAS JEFFERSON, edited by Adrienne Koch and William Peden, Modern Library, Random House, NY, 1944, 1972.

• PLANNED CHAOS by Ludwig von Mises, Foundation for Economic Education, Irvington-on-Hudson, NY, 1947, 1972.
• THEORY AND HISTORY by Ludwig von Mises, Yale University Press, Arlington House, 1957, 1985.
• TIMES ATLAS OF WORLD HISTORY edited by Geoffrey Barraclough, Hammond, Inc., Maplewood, NJ, 1978, 1986.
• UNCLE ERIC TALKS ABOUT PERSONAL, CAREER AND FINANCIAL SECURITY by Richard J. Maybury, Bluestocking Press, Placerville, CA, 1994.
• WHATEVER HAPPENED TO JUSTICE? by Richard J. Maybury, Bluestocking Press, Placerville, CA, 1993.
• WHATEVER HAPPENED TO PENNY CANDY? by Richard J. Maybury, Bluestocking Press, Placerville, CA, 1989, 1991, 1993.
• WORLD ATLAS OF ARCHITECTURE, Mitchell Beazley International Ltd., Great Britain, 1984.

Glossary

AUGUR. Around 600 B.C. in Rome, a soothsayer.

BYZANTINE EMPIRE. The civilization that dominated East Europe, the Mideast and North Africa in the period from roughly 500 A.D. to 1500 A.D. Centered in what is today Turkey. An outgrowth of the Roman Empire, it was loaded with taxes, regulations, welfare programs and a bureaucracy that controlled every facet of economic life.

CAESAR. An emperor of the Roman Empire.

COMMON LAW. The system for discovering and applying the Natural Laws that determine the results of human behavior. The system for discovering and applying the Natural Laws that govern the human ecology. The body of definitions and precedents growing from the two fundamental laws that make civilization possible: (1) Do all you have agreed to do and (2) do not encroach on other persons or their property.

CZAR. Means Caesar. An emperor of the Russian Empire.

DARK AGE. A period of war, economic chaos, persecution, death, destruction, ignorance and terrible poverty.

FASCES. In ancient Rome a bundle of wooden rods bound together by red-colored bands, fixed to a wooden pole topped by an ax. It symbolized the unification of the people under a single government.

FASCISM. The political philosophy that is no philosophy at all, do whatever appears necessary.

GOOSE STEP. A style of marching in which the knees are locked. Very difficult. Signifies extreme militarism and strict obedience to the commands of political leaders.

INAUGURATE. In 600 B.C. Rome, giving magical powers to the king.

INAUGURATION. To bestow with magical powers. The ceremony in which a government official is put in office either to make up laws or to enforce these laws. Dates back to about 600 B.C. Rome.

KAISER. Means Caesar. An emperor of the German Empire.

LATIFUNDIUM. A roman plantation.

PAX ROMANA. The period from 31 BC lasting about 200 years, in which Rome dominated most of Europe, the Mideast and North Africa. The Roman Common Law had created great wealth, and the government could collect enormous taxes to finance its army, forts and roads to conquer the whole Mediterranean world.

POLITICAL UNITY. A large, powerful government that all are forced to obey.

ROMAN DISEASE. Statism. The assumption that laws can be made up by human lawmakers.

ROMAN EMPIRE. The period from roughly 0 to 500 AD in Europe when statism was dominant. It was era of rampant lawmaking, welfare statism, crushing taxes, runaway inflation and war.

ROMAN LAW. The legal system during the Roman Empire. It assumes the individual's rights are granted by the state (by government) and laws can be made up by lawmakers. The state is supreme, and rights are granted or erased whenever lawmakers decide.

ROMAN MONARCHY. From 750 B.C. in Europe until about 500 B.C. when statism was the system. This was when inauguration was invented.

ROMAN MODEL. The legal system that replaced the Roman Common Law. Implies a large central government that all are forced to obey, that can tax and control everything, watchdog everyone's business, and fight wars anywhere on earth. Laws change continually, are arbitrary, and are not based on Higher Law principles. Statism. The opposite of Common Law and Natural Law.

ROMAN REPUBLIC. From 500 B.C. in Europe until about the year 0. An era of abundance and a expansion under an early form of Common Law.

SOCIALISM. An economic and political system under which virtually everything and everyone is owned and controlled by government agencies.

SERFDOM. Economic slavery through heavy taxation.

STATISM. The opposite of the original American philosophy. Assumes political power is a good thing and everyone should have some. Government is our friend, our protector, the solution to our problems. Force is the tool for enforcement. There is no law higher than the government's law.

UNIFIED. See political unity.

About Richard J. Maybury

Richard Maybury, also known as "Uncle Eric," is a world renowned author, lecturer and analyst. He consults with business firms in the U.S. and Europe and is President of Henry Madison Research, Inc. Richard is the former Global Affairs editor of *Moneyworld*, and widely regarded as one of the finest free-market writers in America. Mr. Maybury's articles have appeared in *The Wall Street Journal, USA Today* and other major publications.

His books have been endorsed by top business leaders including former U.S. Treasury Secretary William Simon, and he has been interviewed on more than 200 radio and TV shows across America.

Richard Maybury has penned eleven books in the "Uncle Eric" series and writes an investment newsletter, *U.S. and World Early Warning Report for Investors.*

He has been married for more than 30 years, has lived abroad, traveled around the world, and visited 48 states and 38 countries.

He is truly a teacher for all ages.

Index

Special Offer for Readers of
ANCIENT ROME

As you read each of the "Uncle Eric" books, you will gain a new level of understanding about the world and the turmoil and opportunities that surround us. Many readers find they want updated information from Mr. Maybury and quickly discover they cannot be without his newsletter, *U.S. and World Early Warning Report for Investors.* The publication looks at geopolitics around the globe and how these events will affect you, your family, business and investments. Areas of emphasis include: Chaostan (a term he coined in 1992 – meaning the land of great chaos), the Mideast, the former Soviet Union and Europe.

Readers of *Ancient Rome* are invited to order a sample pack at a reduced price.

This sample pack includes:
1) The most recent issue of *Early Warning Report* newsletter.
2) A detailed map of Chaostan.
3) The six- page special report *Chaostan, The Full Story.*
4) A full color, two-sided, National Geographic map of the world so you can follow events as they unfold.

This is a $35.00 value, but if you call toll free, 1-800-509-5400, Henry Madison Research will send you the sample pack for just $10.00. You can also mail a check for $10.00 to Henry Madison Research, Dept. AR, Box 84908, Phoenix AZ 85071.

Bluestocking Press

Bluestocking Press is the publisher of Richard J. Maybury's "Uncle Eric" series of books and the *Bluestocking Press Catalog* for ages Pre-Kindergarten through adult. The catalog focuses on American history, economics, law and entrepreneurship, all vitally important topics in today's world.

Educated adults realize that learning takes place throughout life. They turn to the *Bluestocking Press Catalog* as a source for information and valuable products for students of all ages. The Bluestocking selection is wide and varied and includes: primary source material, audio history, historical fiction, historical toys, historical music and documents, facsimile newspapers, plus much more.

Visit the Bluestocking Press Catalog online at
BluestockingPress.com

— or —

Order an "Uncle Eric" book today and receive a catalog **FREE** with your order. Or, for first class shipping of the catalog to a U.S. address, mail a check* for $3.00 to:

Bluestocking Press
PO Box 1014 – Dept. AR • Placerville CA 95667 USA

Or, have your credit card ready and phone: 800-959-8586 or 530-621-1123. You can also FAX orders to: 530-642-9222.

Foreign orders are $3.00 for surface shipping or $5.00 for air shipping.

*Make check or money order payable to Bluestocking Press (drawn on a U.S. bank **only** and in U.S. dollars).

Bluestocking Press

"Uncle Eric" Books by Richard J. Maybury

UNCLE ERIC TALKS ABOUT PERSONAL, CAREER & FINANCIAL SECURITY. . . $ 7.95
WHATEVER HAPPENED TO PENNY CANDY? $12.95
WHATEVER HAPPENED TO JUSTICE? $15.95
ARE YOU LIBERAL? CONSERVATIVE? OR CONFUSED? $10.95
ANCIENT ROME: HOW IT AFFECTS YOU TODAY . . . . $ 9.95
EVALUATING BOOKS: WHAT WOULD T. JEFFERSON THINK ABOUT THIS? . . . $ 9.95
THE MONEY MYSTERY . . . . $ 9.95
THE CLIPPER SHIP STRATEGY $15.95
THE THOUSAND YEAR WAR IN THE MIDEAST $17.95
Uncle Eric's Model (SAVE! Includes nine books above) $100.00

Forthcoming "Uncle Eric" Books by Richard J. Maybury

THE WORLD WAR SERIES:
BOOK 10: WORLD WAR I . . . . Contact Bluestocking Press for price
BOOK 11: WORLD WAR II . . . . Contact Bluestocking Press for price

Bluestocking Guides by Jane A. Williams

BLUESTOCKING GUIDE: ECONOMICS—BASED ON RICHARD J. MAYBURY'S BOOK WHATEVER HAPPENED TO PENNY CANDY. Includes: 1) chapter-by-chapter comprehension questions and answers for PENNY CANDY, 2) activities, 3) articles that expand on the concepts presented in WHATEVER HAPPENED TO PENNY CANDY, 4) a list of films that contain good economic history, 5) a final exam and 6) an economic timetable. 125 pages . . . . **$15.95** Study Guides are forthcoming for other "Uncle Eric" books. Query Bluestocking Press for price and availability.

More Bluestocking Press Titles

JONATHAN MAYHEW'S SERMON $4.95
CAPITALISM FOR KIDS. . . . . Contact Bluestocking Press for price
FREE MARKET READER . . . . Contact Bluestocking Press for price
The Bluestocking Press Catalog. . . . . see page 95 for more information

Order information: Order any of the above from Bluestocking Press (see address below). Payable in U.S. funds. Add shipping/handling as follows: Shipping for the first book, add $3.00 (book rate shipping) or $4.00 (foreign orders, surface shipping); shipping for each additional book: add $1.00. Orders shipped to California, please add sales tax.

Prices subject to change without notice.
Confirm prices with publisher before ordering.

Bluestocking Press
P.O. Box 1014 • Dept. AR • Placerville • CA • 95667 • USA
Phone orders: 530-621-1123; 800-959-8586
FAX: 530-642-9222 • BluestockingPress.com